TOP TIPS:
LEADING SMALL GROUPS

Simon Barker and Steve Whyatt

© Scripture Union 2009
First published 2009
ISBN 978 1 84427 388 1

Scripture Union, 207–209 Queensway,
Bletchley, Milton Keynes, MK2 2 EB,
England
Email: info@scriptureunion.org.uk
Website: www.scriptureunion.org.uk

Scripture Union, 157 Albertbridge
Road, Belfast, BT5 4PS
Website: www.suni.co.uk

Scripture Union, 70 Milton St,
Glasgow, G4 0HR
Website: www.suscotland.org.uk

Scripture Union Australia
Locked Bag 2, Central Business Coast
Centre, NSW 2252
Website: www.scriptureunion.org.au

Scripture Union USA
PO Box 987, Valley Forge, PA 19482
Website: www.scriptureunion.org

The right of Simon Barker and Steve
Whyatt to be identified as authors of
this work has been asserted by them
in accordance with the Copyright and
Patents Act 1988.

British Library Cataloguing-in-
Publication Data. A catalogue record
of this book is available from the
British Library.

Printed and bound in Singapore by
Tien Wah Press Ltd.

Logo, cover design, internal design:
www.splash-design.co.uk
Internal illustrations: Colin Smithson
Typesetting: Richard Jefferson, Author
and Publisher Services
Advisers: Paul Cameron, Ems
Hancock, Kathryn Harte.

Scripture Union is an
international Christian charity working
with churches in more than 130
countries, providing resources to bring
the good news of Jesus Christ to
children, young people and families
and to encourage them to develop
spiritually through the Bible and
prayer.

As well as our network of volunteers,
staff and associates who run holidays,
church-based events and school
Christian groups, we produce a wide
range of publications and support
those who use our resources through
training programmes.

CONTENTS

INTRODUCTION

You arrive for the group's meeting only to discover that your co-leader couldn't make it. You know you are in the right place at the right time, but when you arrive only one person is there. Eventually, the rest of the group arrives but two girls have had a disagreement on the way. To be honest, you are not sure what you were meant to be doing and have not done enough preparation... Sound familiar?

We may have a good idea what defines a bad small-group meeting but what about a good one? Where did the idea of small groups come from? Is it just a passing fad in the shift away from everyone sitting at the feet of the expert to a more inter-active approach of learning together through a facilitator? Does the Bible have anything to say about small groups?

Between them, Steve Whyatt and Simon Barker have more than forty years' experience in leading small groups of all ages – from adult home-groups to children's holiday clubs, from school-based Christian groups to young people on residential holidays. Their experience and insights form the basis of this book which is designed to help leaders of small groups for children and young people get a better grasp of why and what they are doing.

Simon and Steve have written this book to equip you to be as good a leader as you possibly can. They are convinced that the community of relationships that you find in a small group is a powerful way to nurture the Christian faith of children and young people.

PART I - WHAT THE BIBLE SAYS 1

Perhaps it is not surprising, but the great commission does not read like this:

...go and make disciples of all nations, baptising them in the name of the Father and of the Son and of the Holy Spirit, and teaching them...*in small groups*...to obey everything I have commanded you!

The Bible says very little specifically about small groups. But we do have the example of Jesus himself and broader principles in the Bible to inspire, guide and challenge us.

Jesus and his relationship with the disciples

When Jesus began his public ministry, one of his first actions was to gather a small group of people around him (Mark 1:16–20; 3:13–19). This was the model of any Jewish leader of the time, enabling less experienced people to hear the leader's wisdom and observe his actions. Thinking ahead to the time when he wouldn't be around, Jesus was choosing to invest in these 12 disciples, not only sharing his insights and teaching but also sharing his very life with them, for three whole years. That was some commitment!

However, this does not mean that the Bible says that 12 is the best number for a small group. Experience would suggest that six to eight is best, to ensure that there are enough people to generate discussion and interaction, while more than eight makes it more difficult to engage every member.

In reality...
'Pete, who leads our Grid group, is always there. I can talk to him and ask him anything and he tells us about himself too. I really trust him.'

Interaction with Jesus (their small-group leader), belonging to a group and absorbing the way that their leader wanted them to live, were all vital parts of the disciples' faith journey as they prepared to continue God's work after Jesus' ascension. Belonging to this group was as important for the disciples as listening to Jesus' stories and teachings or seeing his miracles. (It is interesting that Jesus rarely referred to the disciples as 'disciples', preferring to use terms such as 'brothers' or 'friends'.) By organising them this way, Jesus was giving the early church a model of being his followers, one that was based around a relationship-focused community. 'Community' places people, not programmes, at its heart, where relationships matter far more than the meeting itself.

> **Think about…**
> If spending time together as a group is so important, what can you do to enhance this? Are there tasks you could do together or social outings you could plan?

Jesus lived among his people

Right at the start, from Genesis 1, God is part of a community of Father, Son and Holy Spirit, in relationship together. Although human beings are not part of that unique relationship, we are caught up in it as we relate to the three persons of the Trinity. To find out more, read *Top Tips on Explaining the Trinity to young people* (SU).

From this divine small group, Jesus, the Son, came to live among us. He demonstrated what leading others was all about. This incarnate principle of living alongside people and sharing life is vitally important.

Small groups usually exist for several purposes. This may simply to be a community together, such as a football fan club, sharing common values. Or the purpose may be to perform agreed tasks. These two purposes should exist in the group you lead – to be a community and to perform such tasks as Bible study or supporting each other.

In Mark 6:7–11 and John 13–17, Jesus gave his disciples instructions for the task ahead. But as their leader, he provided for them: he called them his friends (their identity); he washed their feet because they were his disciples (belonging); he gave them insights into the future that they may be confident (security), even though they might not have understood what he was talking about; he promised that the Holy Spirit would be with them for ever (gave direction).

Jesus was honest and acted with integrity. He lived with and through the difficult aspects of relationships such as disagreement (Matthew 20:24), betrayal (Matthew 26:49) and rejection (Matthew 26:56). The most important aspect of Jesus' incarnate role modelling was his total sacrificial investment. Investing in a small group comes at a personal cost to the leader.

The early church way of working

The apostle Peter got up to speak on the day of Pentecost and 3,000 people believed and were baptised! After that we read in Acts 2 that they met together for worship in the Temple and met in homes, where they shared food and fellowship. This was a period of fast numerical growth so the need for nurture and discipleship was vital for faith development. If smaller groups had not been embraced it's difficult to see how growth could have been sustained.

From this early church experience, we can see how meeting together in both large and small groups was vital. In these small groups people broke bread together and shared meals. Food was never far away including celebrating the Lord's supper, all happening in a spirit of 'great joy and generosity' (Acts 2:46). Here was 'spiritual ritual' supplemented with the practical building of relationships, based around the sharing of lives, possessions and meals.

In reality…

Jason, who is 16, said of his cell group at college, 'One of the best things about our group is that we also meet outside of college for pizza, and do other stuff together.'

Small-group community is no less important today, for a child, a young person or an adult member of the church.

Discipling and faith nurture

There are several occasions in the Bible when a wiser person nurtured the faith of another. For example, Jethro and his son-in-law, Moses (Exodus 18), Paul and Silas (Acts 15:39–41) or Priscilla and Aquila with Apollos (Acts 18:26,27). Of course, Jesus himself nurtured the faith of his disciples. Sometimes he took his inner circle to one side, as a small group, such as at the Transfiguration (Mark 9:2–10) or witnessing bringing Jairus' daughter back to life (Mark 5:37–43). All people, but especially children and young people, need places where their faith journey can be explored and experienced – in a formal or informal, large or very small group. The precedent has been set in Scripture. To find out more about nurturing faith, read *Top Tips on Encouraging faith to grow* (SU) – see the inside front cover.

PART TWO – SMALL-GROUP VALUES

2

Purpose

How would you describe the purpose of your small group? Here are some options and more than one may apply at any one time:
- to share a common interest or activity, such as football or drama
- to build quality relationships with each other, leaders and members
- to have fun together
- to nurture faith
- to introduce Jesus to those who know little about him, as in a lunchtime school club
- to provide one of a number of different ways of learning, as in a holiday club, along with up-front presentations, large teams or individual conversation
- to supply the 'community' glue in an activity, giving identity, security and pastoral care, as in a residential holiday

If time is relatively short it can be difficult to build relationships. This can lead to small groups becoming task focused, with little time for sharing, comradeship and pastoral care. The identified purpose of the small group will determine whether being task focused is a problem or not. However, without a

> **Think about…**
> With other group leaders, identify which of these options is your prime purpose.

> **In reality…**
> Ellie, aged 10, couldn't stop talking about her holiday club pod. 'There are six of us and they are now *all* my friends. It's so much fun and we learnt loads about Jesus!' Three important benefits of a group time – learning, fun and relationship.

relationship focus, it is unlikely that a group will develop a dynamic edge, with children and young people keen to contribute.

Distinctly Christian

Of course, small groups are not exclusive to the church and are found in many other settings, such as education, business, sport and leisure, friends and family. But some characteristics are distinctive to a Christian group.

Small groups in a Christian setting usually have some concern for communicating the Christian faith. It has been said many times that the church exists for the benefit of non-members! This might be an exploration of Christianity or some kind of faith nurturing/discipleship or an opportunity to offer Christ's love to others. The purpose is for transformation, that every person moves on in their relationship with God.

Often what motivates the leader in a Christian group is their personal experience of God, wanting to serve others as Jesus did. Such values and purpose for personal involvement can bring stability, longevity, as well as hope. The leader of course is on their journey too, everyone is learning together.

The group reflects some key Christian values, which are also present in any good educational context, as reflected in the outcomes of the government's Every Child Matters agenda: be healthy, be safe, enjoy and achieve, make a positive contribution, achieve economic wellbeing. Christian values in a group might parallel these and seek to create the following:

- A place of acceptance and security for children and young people

- An environment for children and young people to question and learn
- Opportunities for children and young people to explore together
- Care and value of the individual, recognising individual needs and abilities

Any child or young person belonging to a Christian group will experience something quite unique. They will be relating to adults and children whom they may not know well and who may be very different from themselves. In our society, many children's social world is fairly limited to friends of the same age, or with the same interests, or a family group. They can be very wrapped up in themselves. Belonging to a small-group community which has a Christian basis provides an alternative life experience, with a challenge to look beyond themselves into a relational world and ultimately to a relational God.

Stages in the life of a group

Because they are made up of people, communities are dynamic and as such are always changing as people journey through life together. Along with times of group peace and harmony, there are times of difficulty and disharmony. These times are normal and should be embraced as much as times of celebration. There are many stages in the life of a small-group community. Here are five of them:

Stage one: Initiation

This happens especially when the group is first formed. People get to know one another. Icebreaker and fun name games can facilitate this. The leader's role is important in creating the environment and group identity and in setting the agenda. Does the leader exercise control and authority or operate with a more fluid approach? How far does the leader share their own life with group members at this stage? To some extent, the small-group's identity will reflect something of who the

In reality…

'I was very nervous when I arrived at XcellR8 (a residential weekend) as I didn't know anyone. But we soon got into groups and played a game which helped me get to know Naomi. I didn't feel worried after that.'

leader is and their ambition for the group. These issues of initiation need to be visited regularly, for example when new people join or at the start of a new term.

Stage two: Wrangling

As a group gets established, members jostle for position and status. It can be difficult for a leader since the group task, such as Bible engagement, is the last thing on anyone's agenda. Being aware that this is happening enables a leader to be patient and firm. This

In reality…

On the Monday of the holiday club, Lisa was always pushing herself to the front and never listening, while Jack was on the fringe. Their roles had completely reversed by Friday.

wrangling is particularly evident with young people but can occur with children. Although most likely following initiation, it does occur at other times.

Stage three: Settling and functioning

A sense of common ground has been found which gives a platform for everyone to build relationships and meet the agreed task of the group. Don't expect this to last for ever.

Stage four: Growth

A settled group leads to growth. Individual members as well as the group as a whole, begin to thrive. The efficiency of the group is high and the sense of belonging, ownership and achievement develops. As the opportunities for further growth expand, this can demand more time and energy from the leader.

Stage five: Transformation

In the Christian context the expectation is that God will transform lives. So, the small group has become the catalyst for God to work. The leader is privileged to observe what is going on and to play an appropriate part. It is always a good idea to evaluate after every session where there has been change and development with individuals and as a whole. It is always best to keep a record, since it is easy to forget. Measuring the success of a session might include numbers, impressions of how the session went, or how well you delivered the content. Most important though is how the group was transformed.

The pace of transformation will depend on factors such as

In reality...
'Only three people came this week but they must have been the three whom God wanted to be there. They interacted so well – it was quite unique. We never got onto the material I had prepared, but that's OK!'

how often a group meets, the make up of the group, the extent of the leader's commitment and, of course, the work of the Holy Spirit.

Learning together

The group leader, using the traditional 'chalk and talk' education model, is seen as the 'fount of all knowledge', imparting wisdom to attentive listeners. However a variety of different models of learning, most of which are more participative, have now been recognised. These are largely based on the small-group model. Students work in smaller groups (not always the same groups) around a task or challenge, and communication (collaborative learning) between students is actively encouraged. 'Speaking and listening' are education buzz words. The teacher becomes the facilitator for the learning experience.

The principle of learning together is to be embraced in small groups as leaders and members learn together. This means that a leader needs to be open to new ideas and ways of thinking, as well as embracing the vulnerability that accompanies such openness. The small group becomes not so much a place that provides answers, as a safe place for questions, to learn in partnership and share experiences together.

In effect, the leader has become a facilitator, a role model, a carer and a questioner as opposed to an up-front leader or teacher. These latter roles may still sometimes be appropriate when clear information and guidance are needed. Of course, the leader then has to ensure that everyone has understood the information, seeing its relevance to their own lives.

Small groups are also unique places for children and young people to experience and explore leadership. Cell groups are generally peer led, such as Christian groups in schools (Christian Unions). There are prayer groups in schools led by primary school children or residential weekends

where 80% of the programme is delivered by young people. This is not to negate the presence of adults in small groups but is a challenge to think what is possible within a small group.

The adult leader is not only a role model but also an intentional facilitator, there to enable the development of the children's gifts. A leader should not end up like a superbly skilled footballer who rarely passes the ball to teammates! The teammates may admire this player but are frustrated because they never get a chance to excel, let alone score a goal.

In reality...

'To be honest I don't see my role as Sunday school "teacher". I think I learn more from them than they from me!'

Questions

If someone asked Jesus a question, he often responded with a question of his own. He was recognising the need for people to think and learn for themselves. Question-based learning is an important focus in schools because it develops thinking skills. It's an important part of any group leadership.

Think about…

'Good questions rarely require answers, just lots of thought and comment! Indeed answers can often ruin a question's power and reduce a group's learning opportunity.'

Of course, asking questions also calls for listening. Jesus didn't just respond to what was said verbally, but sometimes he responded to what was not verbalised. For example, in John 4:1–26 Jesus talked with the woman at the well. He began with a request for a drink, but then responded to the woman's comments and unspoken needs. Good questioning and listening skills are a great asset and are skills that can be developed.

Preparing questions is always useful but sometimes there is a need to digress. Ask questions in the right way, and watch your group take off. Ask the wrong questions in the wrong way and the silence can be deafening!

1 Closed questions: these usually require either a simple yes or no answer which can be helpful in making decisions or establishing facts. (Was anyone else with Jesus when he met the woman?)

2 Factual questions: these require the reader to examine what has been written. (In the story, how many husbands did the woman have?)

3 Open questions: these are more effective in developing discussion and encouraging people to open up and share thoughts and feelings. (What do you think the woman thought when Jesus said that?)

4 Hypothetical questions: these can be used to encourage further discussion as well as a more personal response. (If you were in the woman's shoes, what would you have done?)

5   Reflective questions: these are used to reflect back what someone has said. This can be done to check understanding (Are you saying that the woman was surprised by what Jesus said to her?). Or to reflect back what the speaker or group might be feeling (I get the impression you are amazed at how Jesus knew so much about this woman. Am I right?).

Non-verbal communication includes body language or tone and volume of voice, all important in small-group dynamics. Even the person who says nothing verbally is communicating something! The position someone sits in or whether people have an open or closed posture communicates very loudly!

External circumstances such as what is going on at home or school have an impact on how your small group listens and responds to questions and comments. Pastoral needs of individual members are always significant so you need God's wisdom to know just how prominent they are in any one group time. Listen with ears and eyes!

In answering an unexpected question, reply with 'That's a good question,' followed by asking the questioner what they think and then ask the rest of the group. If appropriate, admit if you don't know the answer, but promise to find out for next time. To find out about helping children and young people explore together what the Bible says, read *Top Tips on Discovering the Bible with children* and *Exploring the Bible with young people* (SU) – see inside front cover.

Behave, believe, belong

'Behave, believe, belong' are three steps associated with what is required for anyone to be a part of church community. But which comes first? Do children and young people need to behave, and then believe if they are going to belong? The three steps in the order above emphasise the need for a newcomer to conform, changing their behaviour as well as values and beliefs before they can be sure they are accepted. There is no recognition that belonging to a group may bring about change in beliefs and behaviour.

'Belong, believe, behave', however, has a different starting point. A young person does not have to conform to ensure that they belong to a small-group community. Group members find their place in this community and together everyone explores belief and behaviour. This is more challenging for a leader but values the individual far more and in the long-term is more effective. Of course, not every group member goes on to 'believe and behave'.

In the stages of a group's life, members may communicate (explicitly or implicitly) that the person isn't really welcome any more which reverts back to the model of 'behave, believe, belong', as though the belonging was conditional on believing or behaving in an acceptable way. But all are welcome as unique individuals if a small-group community is based on genuine relationships, without defining exactly how God will be at work. A wise leader will ensure that the well-being of all members are met.

PART THREE - PRACTICAL IDEAS

3

In an ideal world, if you were leading a small group you might want to choose who was in it, where and when it met, how long meetings lasted and what activities went on. But welcome to the real world! In all likelihood, these choices have already been made for you. This may make you feel somewhat resigned and powerless. The following guidelines should enable your group to function effectively even if you are meeting in a broom cupboard with ten hyperactive 7-year-olds!

Being a small-group leader

Consider your role within the group. You may be some of the following:

- Friend – to get alongside group members and build relationships
- Teacher – to be entrusted with imparting some biblical truths and spiritual lessons
- Facilitator – to chair or facilitate a discussion/activity where everyone can contribute
- Parent – to insist on a matter of health, safety or personal hygiene

Group members look to their leader as a role model and so it is important that before you become a leader, you are sure that your own relationship with God is secure and that your lifestyle outside of the group reflects that faith.

Working with a co-leader

It is always helpful to work with a co-leader. You may need to leave the room to get resources or see what has happened to the person who went to the toilet five minutes ago! It helps to pray with someone else, to plan and prepare together and deliver those parts of the programme that suit your experience/personality. (Some leaders hate drama or crafts while others love them!) Afterwards you can review the session together. Make sure that you:

- are quite clear about the aims and who is responsible for which elements
- have a working knowledge of all the activities just in case your co-leader is ill or suddenly required elsewhere

Preparation

Your priorities need to be Preparation, Preparation, Preparation. As the saying goes, 'Fail to prepare, prepare to fail'. There are various phases to this, most of which need to be done weeks or days before you meet (rather than minutes and seconds):

Personal preparation

Find out all you can about who is in the group and any particular issues or points of contact.

It is always helpful to talk with someone who understands your age

In reality…

On the first day of the holiday club, Sarah welcomed a Polish girl into the group. That evening she went onto the Internet to find out a few Polish words and even printed out the words of the Learn and remember verse in Polish.

group, such as a teacher, experienced youth worker or parent and pick their brains! Show them what you are planning and ask for advice.

Prayer

Pray for group members regularly and individually. Pray for them by name if at all possible but, if not, picture them in your mind as you pray. Pray for each group time and for your co-leader.

Philosophy

Find out what are the key aim(s) of the group. These may vary from day-to-day. Do you want to get to know one another? Is it about delivering the key teaching of the day or re-enforcing some teaching from elsewhere? Do you want to enable children to work out how truths in the Bible affect their lives or to help children pray together? What about preparing a drama or craft idea that will be required later in the programme? Is it time out just to relax and have fun? Being sure of the expected outcome will shape what happens.

Practical

Find out where your group will meet. How will you set up the venue? What equipment will you need and is it immediately available? How long will you have? Read through any Bible passages and prepare any activity sheets or questions. Look back to page 16 to be reminded of the sorts of questions you might ask. If there is a craft to be made, make one yourself in advance. Will your age group be able to cope or do you need to do some extra preparation such as cutting out? What activities will you drop if time is tight so that you still include the key teaching points? What will you do if they get through the material and you have five minutes to fill? Some suggested fillers are on page 30.

The group time

The meeting place

Whether you meet in a large hall, a gazebo or a dedicated room, create a space that is 'yours'. The group could decorate it with posters, flags or rugs. Think carefully about storage of bags, coats, Bibles or pens and where you will keep work that is collected at the end. Is there space to sit in a circle so everyone can see each other? Do chairs help or hinder?

In reality…

'Our holiday club den had 'walls' made of chairs but we covered them with painted cardboard, put rugs on the floor and made a low arch for everyone to crawl inside. It was brilliant and it was ours!'

If you are outside, who will be facing the sun? Are there any visual distractions you could easily avoid? What about the needs of anyone with a disability?

Circle time

Sitting in a circle (or oval) so that everyone can see each other is ideal because it helps everyone to feel included and, if possible, the leader should be on the same level as everyone else. You may all sit on the floor but if, for example, you have someone in a wheelchair, it may be better for everyone to have a chair. If you are in a noisy venue it may be better for the group to lie on the floor, faces inwards, forming a star shape as this makes it easier to hear and be heard. To ensure listening, it helps if only the person holding an agreed object speaks at any one time.

Prayer

You will want to encourage times of prayer in your group. Some people may be confident to pray in a group setting but for the less confident you could pass an object around the group and anyone who does not want to pray out loud holds the object for a moment in silence and then passes it on. Of course, not all prayer needs to be spoken and pictures, writing, objects and music can all be valuable prayer tools. See *Top Tips on Prompting prayer* (SU) for prayer ideas.

Bible

Reading a Bible passage around a circle, one verse each, helps everyone feel included and ensures that everyone has found the right passage! But some children do not like to read aloud, others struggle with reading, some have very quiet voices and there may be several different Bible versions to cause confusion. Reading round in a group inevitably breaks up the flow of a passage or story.

Options include:

- giving a time of quiet for people to read it to themselves
- asking for volunteers to read aloud
- asking confident readers to read aloud
- reading it aloud yourself

- print out the passage on sheets of paper, then everyone has the same version and the text can be laid out so it is easy to read. Use highlighter pens so that different people can read (or act!) out different parts. If you use this approach, it is strongly recommended that you do a follow-up activity that requires the group to open and use their own Bibles because finding a Bible passage is an important skill to develop. Young people need to see Bible passages in their context, not in isolation.

People in the group

Whenever possible, set up the meeting place before anyone arrives so that you are not hassled. Be there to welcome everyone by name and set the tone for what is to follow. If you are going to be delayed, make suitable provision. (Why not put instructions for the first task in a sealed envelope saying 'To be opened by the person with the longest surname' or '… birthday nearest to March 20'.)

The group members

Each group will be made up of unique individuals but on the next page are a few stereotypes… along with ideas for dealing more effectively with them!

With each of these types, try to grab 20 seconds outside the group time to chat 1-2-1, saying such things as: 'Little Miss Know-it-all, it's great that you know all the answers but could you help me today by letting others have a go first,' 'Little Mr Fidget, if you manage not to annoy X, then you can have first choice of biscuit today,' 'Little Miss Silent, are you enjoying the group time? Would it be OK if I asked you to read a Bible verse today?'

Character	Characteristic	Your tactic
Little Miss Know-it-all	Answers every question in full before anyone else says a word.	Specifically address questions to other group members.
Little Mr Fidget	Can't sit still. Fidgets with equipment and constantly prods his neighbours.	Use him for tasks such as giving out equipment. Sit next to him.
Little Miss Disinterested	Moody. Not getting involved.	Don't worry immediately – it's probably not you. Find a minute for a 1-2-1 chat.
Little Mr Talkative	Chats constantly, sometimes about what is being discussed but frequently not.	Use tasks that involve going round the group in turn. Sit opposite him so you have good eye contact.
Little Miss Silent (not to be confused with Little Miss Disinterested)	Is paying attention and involved but doesn't contribute verbally.	Accept it – she may be naturally quiet and shy. Gently encourage some participation as time goes on.

Discipline

- Expect, positively affirm and reward good behaviour: 'Well done for...'; 'Thanks for...'
- Build up the group identity so that any bad behaviour is not seen as personal conflict: 'In this group we...' This is particularly important if a child displays behaviour which is either tolerated or promoted at home. Never undermine the parents' position but explain that such behaviour is not what is expected here.
- Position yourself to have eye contact with all members and use non-verbal signals that encourage positive behaviour such as a raised eyebrow, a finger to your lips, a restraining hand on the fidgeting knee.
- Have a range of small but significant rewards such as being the person who collects the pencils or who can get their drink first.
- Know what sanctions are available in the event of continued disruptive behaviour. (Is there a 'Time Out' area? Do they need to be seen by a senior leader? Does a letter need to go to parents?)

The mix

Mixed gender

Single sex groups are very different to mixed ones. Research suggests that girls tend to do better in school in single sex classes whereas boys do better in mixed ones. Without falling into sexual stereotypes, it is generally acknowledged that more girls enjoy (and so learn through) activities that involve reading and writing (and neat colouring!) whereas boys tend to learn better through doing – games, drama and certain construction activities – though boys can enjoy puzzles and code cracking.

Mixed learning styles

The many different learning styles and preferences are spread across both genders. As far as possible, adapt the programme to include a variety of activities to cater for a wide range of learning styles.

Mixed church experience

One young person may have a fully rounded theology on predestination while another may not have even heard the story of the cross. In a widely diverse group, a leader can pitch material in the middle and end up satisfying very few. If this is a group where non-churched children are likely to be involved for only a limited time (eg holiday club or summer camp) it makes sense to use any Christian young people present to share their faith and knowledge with others. In a longer-term setting (Sunday group, School club) it may be better to occasionally have a distinct focus one way or to provide a range of response options for use after some shared material.

Mixed ages

Churches with a small number of children often attempt to run a group that caters for ages as wide as 5 to 15. Experience says that anything more than a three-year range in a group can bring challenges. In this situation, a variety of tasks and activities are needed and while you may all gather together for a Bible story, you will need to break into much smaller units for age-appropriate response or follow-up activities.

Mixed ability

Even a group with a small age range will contain a range of abilities – academic, artistic or sporting. No one blueprint will meet all needs but ensure (ideally) that within your time together each individual is

supported through any area of weakness and is given the opportunity to excel in an area of strength.

Special needs

Your group may include one or more person with special needs. These may be immediately obvious (eg a child in a wheelchair) or more subtle (eg an ADHD child who arrives one day without having taken their medication). In all situations:

- Try to discover the exact nature of the need from the parent/carer or children themselves.
- Look for the positives – what can they do? What are they good at?
- Understand the limitations – what can't they do? What will they struggle with?

Your event should have a Special Needs Coordinator (or someone designated to help in this area). Ask for their assistance, perhaps in amending activity sheets or redesigning activities. Aim to work towards inclusion, making changes that will make as much of your time accessible to all the children in the group.

Safeguarding yourself and the children

Safeguarding yourself

Caring for children or young people is a very important task. If you have any responsibility for a group of children or young people your organiser should ensure that you are appropriately vetted through CRB/ISA and have received appropriate training.

Safeguarding children

Being a group leader is likely to make you someone whom children and young people come to trust and confide in. For the most part this will require nothing more than a listening ear and some friendly advice. Sometimes it may be appropriate to pray with an individual if they are willing. On occasions, however, a child may share with you a situation which requires further action. Your event should have a Child Protection policy and your organiser should have briefed you on what to do should such a situation arise but the following are key points:

- Never promise confidentiality to a child. You have a legal obligation to pass certain information on.

- Stay with a child until they are calm.

- Never ask questions which seek for information; rather, listen carefully and seek only clarification.

- Do not comment on whether you believe a child or not. The fact they have shared with you means that there is an issue that requires action whether their comments subsequently turn out to be true or not.

- Only speak about this to those who have the responsibility for dealing with such issues. Never speak about it with anyone who may be implicated, no matter how well known they are to you.

- As soon as is possible, write down exactly what was said.

- Seek prayer for yourself from someone with whom you can share just outline details.

Filler ideas

As a group leader there will always be odd moments when you are asked (often without warning) to fill an extra five minutes. You need a bank of ideas to draw on immediately. Older children are more likely to be happy just to sit and chat but for younger ones, try these:

- Ask each group member to say (or draw) what they would have for a birthday meal treat.
- Ask each group member to describe their ideal day on holiday/their best holiday.
  (Both these and similar ideas can also be used in an 'I went to the market and bought…' memory game.)
- Everyone tells or writes their favourite (clean!) joke on a Post-it note and gives it to a leader or just have a joke book to hand.
- Play a few rounds of a game such as Simon Says or the Yes/No Game (answering questions without saying yes or no).
- Have a mental puzzle which the children can only solve by asking questions to which you can answer yes or no. Ideas include:
  (Q) How did a carrot, a scarf and five pieces of coal come to be found in the middle of a field when no one was around? (A) The snowman had melted.
  (Q) How come the owner of a Rolls Royce was declared bankrupt when his car pulled up outside a hotel? (A) He was playing Monopoly.
- Hold one end of a ball of wool and, sitting in a circle, throw the ball to a group member who catches it, calls out, say, his favourite TV show, holds the wool strand and throws the ball onto someone else. Eventually a spider's web is built!

TEN TOP TIPS

- Pray for your group and don't forget the reason why your group exists

- Be familiar with the child protection policy of your church or organisation

- Prepare your material

- Set up your venue to suit your needs

- Aim to be inclusive of everyone in building a sense of community

- Know which activities are central to your time and focus on those

- If the Bible is being used, ensure everyone has one and uses one

- Deal with problems in 1-2-1 conversations where possible

- Seek help from others if you are struggling

- Stay positive. It's better to 'achieve' less and enjoy it, than create tension in trying to complete everything.

RESOURCES

General guidance
Pretty much everything you need to know about... series
Draper, Franklin and O'Shea, *Working with 5–7s*, SU, 2007
Saunders and Porritt, *Working with 8–10s*, SU, 2004
Williams and Stephenson, *Working with 11–14s*, SU, 2004
Danny Brierly, *Young people and small groups*, SU, 1998
Phil Green, *Synergy – The ultimate cell group guide*, Kevin Mayhew, 2002

Programmes for groups
www.schoolslive.org – a wealth of free downloadable resources for anyone leading a school Christian group
www.lightlive.org – a wealth of free downloadable resources for anyone leading a church-based group for children or young people

Various *SUbstance* Volumes 1 to 5, SU, 2008, 2009 (for 14–18s)
Word-Up series, SU (small group Bible study for 11–14s)

Eyelevel midweek club resources
Sharp and Derry, *Streetwise*, SU, 2003
Sue Clutterham, *Awesome*, SU, 2004
Steve Hutchinson, *So, Why God?* SU, 2007
Mary Moody, *Target Challenge*, SU, 2008
Ro Willoughby, *Dress Rehearsal*, SU, 2009

Holiday club resources
Helen Franklin, *Champion's Challenge*, SU, 2007
Ruth Wills, *Showstoppers*, SU, 2008
Dave Godfrey, *Rocky's Plaice*, SU, 2009